I0527902

# in the dark

## A COLLECTION OF POEMS
## BY DONDRIA

AWE ME
ENTERTAINMENT

*in the dark*

ISBN: 979-8-218-30115-6

Artwork by Rious Photography | riousshotme.com

AWE ME ENTERTAINMENT, LLC

3900 Crown Rd SW
#16709 SMB#33309
Atlanta, GA 30304

This book is dedicated to you, Dear Reader.
Let this collection of poems be a reminder that even at
your worst, you have purpose and you are loved. You are
such an important part of this multiverse and I appreciate
you. You got this.

Light and Love, Dondria

# Preface

The majority of my career was a cycle of me giving my power away. I was severely unfamiliar with autonomy and how to acquire my own. I can partially blame it on the fact that I just didn't know any better. I was a sheltered girl from the suburbs who got plucked off the internet and thrown into the music industry. I didn't know what I wanted to do, who I wanted to be, or how I wanted to sound. I hadn't gotten a chance to discover myself. So it was easy to trust those with experience. I was open to being guided and groomed.

But once I assumed the position of an independent artist, it hit me... I had no idea who I was. I had no vision or plan for my life. I just accepted that my career had run its course and I'd be pivoting soon.

In walks a man who specialized in smoke and mirrors. He promised to help me pick myself up, dust myself off, and become who I was meant to be. Instead, he isolated me from my support system, forced his own vision for my career on me, verbally and mentally abused me, and violated my trust time and time again. I was miserable.
How did I go from bad to worse?

As depression and anxiety began to settle in, I would sit in my closet, open my journal, and use poetry (and prayer) as an outlet for my intrusive thoughts and a desperate plea for a brighter tomorrow. This collection of poems lead me through the darkness and into the light.

# Introduction

Depression is common.

About 280 million people worldwide have depression, including 5 percent of the world's adults and 5.7 percent of adults above the age of 60. Like an uninvited guest, depression made itself at home within my heart and mind also. I found solace in seeking professional help, getting my prayer on and pouring my thoughts onto paper.

As you turn the pages of "In The Dark," let the verses serve as a reminder that hope is not lost, and a better tomorrow awaits those who dare to seek it. Together, we shall conquer the darkness, hand in hand, through the power of words, self-discovery, and the unwavering belief that healing is possible. May this book serve as a companion to your own voyage towards the light.

In the final pages of this book, you will find blank sheets, waiting to bear the weight of your thoughts. Let the ink flow like a river, carrying away any negativity that haunts your mind.

# You are NOT alone.

If you're feeling overwhelmed by painful and unbearable thoughts, know you don't have to manage them alone. Trained crisis counselors can offer compassionate support by talking through your feelings and exploring options for more support.

Reach out and connect by:
- calling 988 to reach the <u>National Suicide Prevention Lifeline</u>
- texting HOME to 74I-74I to reach the <u>Crisis Text Line</u>

# Acknowledgements

I give thanks to God, my creator, who chose me to live this life. There's NO WAY I would be here without supernatural protection and provision.

I'm so incredibly grateful to my family and friends who have seen me and loved me along this journey.

I'd like to acknowledge my parents: Rodney and Cynthia McCarty & Joel and Tonya Fields for reminding me from day one that the sky is the limit.

Thank you to my incredible soon-to-be husband Demetrious for loving all parts of me and being the most supportive partner I could ever dream of.

To Robin Kindrick, thank you for your invaluable sisterhood and mentorship. I can always count on you to help me come up with a plan to make any dream of mine become a reality; this book is no different.

And lastly, to the best fans in the world: you all have been the most amazing supporters as I've navigated through my music career and explored other avenues of expression. I appreciate you.

## May God bless you all.

The shadow is the greatest teacher for how to come to the light.

-Ram Dass

Table of Contents

in the dark [part one]

in my dreams [part two]

IN THE DARK

dans le noir...

In the dark

IN THE DARK

en la oscuridad...

in the dark

n the dark
ark the in
he dark in

IN THE D.

nell'oscurità...

In the dark

in the dark

# in the dark

## (part one)

*In The Dark*

I'm thirty-something and still afraid of the dark.
I still keep a night light and leave the tv on.

I'm afraid of the dark, not for its absence of light,
but because I know what lurks in its depths.
It's here where I must confront the things that I've buried
deeper than any treasure you could find.
It's here where my fears take shape and shadows dance with my
mind.

There is, however, a small flicker of light in the distance.
It whispers to me that night is not eternal;
the sun will shine again.
It tries to remind me that in the dark,
exists the potential for a miracle.
And, in facing our demons,
we discover they aren't even ours to claim.
We discover our strength, our resilience,
our capacity for change.

But what if fear is louder?
What if it clings to you like a weight,
pulling you deeper into the abyss.
Taunting you like a mirage in the desert.
Leading you close to the light but never close enough.

I close my eyes and take a deep breath.
Try to muster the courage to face what lies ahead.
Yeah, I know that only by facing the demons can I ever hope to
find the light. But I'm not ready yet.

I'm thirty-something and still afraid of the dark.

*Masks*

We wear these masks.
To display only what we want them to see.

To disguise our depressions.
Our unhealthy obsessions.
Our need to be accepted.

We wear these masks.

To hide our true beings.
To keep our opinions.
And fall into submission.

We wear these masks.

To safeguard our hearts.
For too many times they've been split apart.

So forgive me for blotting out the very things that make
me, me.

Until assurance is assured,
You'll never see the real me.

Broken

It's her personality. Her smile. Her spirit, they say.
I'm the girl who brightens people's days.

The reason people smile though it's dark and gloomy.
The Optimist. The Child of God. The Motivator.
The Inspiration.

I'm The Great Pretender.

I pretend I'm happy 24 hours a day.
I break the purest hearts,
and deceive the most innocent minds.
I bury my misery so deep,
I couldn't excavate it if I tried.

I sit at home in solitude,
content with the emptiness caused by leeches.
I can make you think I've cured you, my fangs penetrating,
as I molest your weaknesses.

I wish my God would mend these broken pieces.

The imminence of time intensifies my insanity
and my once rapid heartbeat is beginning to flat line.

Where do I begin with mending this broken heart?
Every time I lift the needle to sew it back together,
I tear off another part.

I put ice on the bruises, it just makes me cold.
I sprinkle positivity on my wounds,
but wickedness takes ahold.

I wish God would fix this brokenness.
Make me whole again. Give me a new heart.
I wish I could unlock these chains of guilt and hurt,
shame and defeat, fear, self-doubt and uncertainty.

Days Like Today

Days like today.

I wish I could sleep the day away to suppress my fears...
Stay in the house to avoid the inevitability of failure.
After all, you can't lose if you don't try.

Days like today.

I'd rather turn off my phone,
neglecting all responsibilities.

Elude love rather than savor the sweetness of its process.

Cry before the pain comes, if it even comes,
to mitigate heartache later.

When you feel nothing's worth fighting for.
When you feel you're not worth fighting for.

Days like today.

I've given so much of myself to them,
there's nothing left for me.

I've stretched myself so thin,
my existence now feels subjective.

In my brokenness, I've hurt the ones who loved me most,
and now I'm stuck with the fake and unidentifiable.

Days like today.

When it's easier to live a lie than walk in truth.

When you lack the courage to look in the mirror and admit
your faults.

When you lack the confidence to look in the mirror and
admit your strengths.

Days like today.

*Good Man*

They say love is hard to find.
But a good man is harder.

Someone who treats you kind,
someone you can be a part of something good with.

It's difficult for you to find the one who sees you the way
you do... the one who treats you like your flaws ain't
issues. Who's not afraid to say they've missed you.

I need a good man.

Someone who speaks my love language.
Understands my uncertainties.
Who's willing to get down on one knee.

I need a good man.

*Hate Sleeping Alone*

I exchanged my California King for a full
assuming it would be easier to sleep alone.
It's not.

Now I'm forced to lie in my tears...
I can no longer scoot to the dry side.

And I still shiver.
In fetal position on those cold nights.
Yearning for his body heat... or anyone's for that matter.

Because I hate sleeping alone.

For when I sleep alone, I'm forced to face my demons.
And battle the haunting specters of depression and self-
pity.

I can no longer hide underneath a man until my nightmare of
a reality is diverted by deep slumber.

So tonight, as I close my eyes,
I'll try to resist the urge to cry.
But if I do shed a few, I pray the Lord sees me through.

I hate sleeping alone.

13

More

Why do you do what you do?

Never mind your sense of humor and good looks,
what helps you suspend your consciousness at night?
What do you think about in the shower after a long day?
What fills you with passion?

Forget the fact that I'm easy on the eyes with a hint
conviviality, what draws your soul to mine?

What's your motivation when the sun rises?

These are the things I long to know.
These are the sides I wish you'd show.

Your wall of mystery prevents me from kissing your dreams
goodnight and your fears away.

How is there esoteric gain when you keep me at bay?
Why do you do that thing I hate?

My need for more and your neglect in fulfilling reminds me
of a story with a tragic end.

And so my Dear, I bid you adieu.
And hope one day, if its not too late,
you'll see the light and discover your muse.

*I Miss You*

I Miss You.

She fights sending that simple text everyday.

She knows it's not good for her.
She's been weaning herself off this lack of a man for
months now.

Why does he still have a hold on her mind, body, and soul?
How is it that one scroll drags her back to excusing all
the times he hurt her?

"What's one text? It's not like I'm gonna end up back in
bed with him".

So she sends it...

Part-Time Lover

I'll only need you sometimes...
The Winter and Fall.
I'll give a little of me...
But never my all.

I need a part-time lover who won't require much,
Doesn't ask questions or need more than my touch.

No feelings, no I love you's.
No check-ins, jealous eyes.
Just good weed n great sex.
Your body on mine.

Dear Part-Time Lover,
Please don't commit to me.
A little goes a long way.
A taste is all I need.

*Void*

Won't you fill my void?
Fill my empty space
Captivate my mind
Bury pain I can't bear to face

Won't you be my drug?
Help me fantasize
Blur my mental
Numb my brain
Feed me with your lies

I'd rather be your temporary
than a nonexistent being.
I'd rather be your adversary
than a stranger with no meaning.
I'd rather be your whenever, than never at all.
Believing all your falsities, answering every call.

Won't you fill my void?
Enable my delusion
Deem me helplessly in love
Enhancing my confusion

I'd rather have a piece of what it could've been...

Even if it exists only in my dreams.

Denial

He doesn't want me, but he says he does.

He says all the right things,
and half of the time his actions agree.

The other half makes me question why he's even here.
Is it my warm honeypot he can't keep his hands out of?
My light from within everyone takes a piece of?
Is my lack of confidence evidence he can control my
thoughts and emotions?
Or all of the above?

He says all the right things,
and at least half of the time his actions agree.

Am I settling for less or are my expectations too high?
Am I riding the wave of insanity in hopes he'll become the
one for me?

He doesn't want me, but he says he does.
And I know it.

Yet I'll stay right here.
Where it's safe.
Where it's familiar.

In denial.

Taken

He's everything I ever wanted in a man.

Tall, dark, and handsome.
Intelligent, loving, and kind.
When he looks into the windows of my soul,
I know it's real.

But he's only mine in my mind.
Because he's taken.

I can tell I make him happy.
Better than anyone ever could.
He shares with me his dreams, his fears.
I share the secrets that bring me to tears.

We have a bond that can't be broken.

But he's only mine in my mind.
Because he's taken.

'A' needs a healing only I can give.
Her heart is so cold, her pain evident.
I yearn to restore her, make her whole again.

'B' fulfills me. Mind, body, and soul.
She brings forth a healing no one ever could.
She does for me what sun and water do for the Lily.
She gives me the strength and courage to change the world.

But my only objective is 'A'.

'A' is so damaged, so broken... mostly because of me.
I owe her the cure of love and affection.
But my cup is empty.
And 'A' can't refill it.

So I'm addicted to 'B'. She completes me.
Opens my eyes to who I could be. What I'm capable of.
My potential.

As I'm selfishly fulfilled, they're selflessly neglected.
And what's serving me is wounding the collective.

My confusion is leading 'B' towards resentment and 'A' deeper
into her hole.

And I'm stuck in the middle with no relief from this tangled web
I wove.

Infidelity

There are 3 sides to every story.

He's looking to fill a void but doesn't know how to
communicate.

She's too blinded by their facade to notice
she helped to create.

And the mistress? Well, her lack of confidence and self-worth
makes her susceptible to anything that lies, cheats, and
steals if it _sounds_ like love and affection.

Together they create a whirlwind of shame and deception.

Ruining whatever's in its path... person, place, or thing.
Including the children.

One act of selfishness turns into a year's worth of
dishonesty, disappointment, and ultimate delusion.

She's no longer in the dark about her other half.
She knows he's a liar and a cheat.
But because he keeps a roof over her head and Giuseppe on her
feet, she saves her tears for when she's alone.

She weeps not because 'she gave him her all
and how dare he repay her this way' --
She cries because if this gets out, her picture perfect
family will be exposed for what it really is…
a joke.

So I year turns into 2, and 2 into 3.

3 into an illegitimate baby and a mixed family with a deliberate explanation as to why Ashley and James have a new baby sister that their mother didn't carry, a stretched thin paycheck due to the extra mouth to feed...

and still the void lingers.

Poison

Your kiss was so misleading.
I didn't know your fangs had penetrated my delicate skin
until I was lying on my deathbed.

Your sweet lies graced my ears
with the most beautiful song.
They entered my canal, encompassed my brain,
and traveled to my labia.

Before your hands ever touched my body,
your warm tones had me hypnotized,
mesmerized as I fantasized about you and I.

You had me right where you wanted me.
As the thoughts, "I think I love him" stirred up in my
mind, that was your cue to go in for the kill.

Your venom stung just right as it flowed through my veins.
It was exhilarating.
I was 16 again on my first marijuana high.

You whispered more distractions and made love to me until I
fell asleep.

Now here I lay, awaken yet paralyzed.
Oblivious to the silent streams flowing from my eyes.

Numb from your poison.

Numb

What does pain even feel like anymore?
What are the signs of a broken heart?
What does it feel like to be hurt to the core?

I've been walking this road of lethargy for so long,
my stride has become robotic.
I witness others' expressions
and wonder why I'm not as melodic.

Why their tears fall like raindrops
and mine have turned to stone.
Why they long for one to hold and I'd rather be left alone.

Is it as simple as someone applying oil to my rusty heart?
Or will it take a lifetime to chip away at the wall it took
a lifetime to build?

What does pain even feel like anymore?
What does it feel like
to have your heart ripped out of your chest?
Will I ever know?

Or will I continue to escape the pain,
eventually becoming the inflictor,
polluting another's veins?

Numb.

# in my dreams

## (part two)

Diamond

I've been picked at and pressured.
Bumped and bruised.
Squeezed and stabbed.
A spectacle to peruse.
But Mama, I made it.

I've been lied on, robbed.
Manipulated and abused.
Laughed at, given up on.
Corrupted and misused.
But Mama, I made it.

That pressure made a diamond.
That pressure made me strong.
That pressure made me wise.
And I'mma keep keepin' on.

You mad?

Destiny

Destiny.
The predetermined, usually inevitable or
irresistible, course of events.

I have one.
Before I was born, God planned it out.
Never has a soul been conceived without.

But with destiny comes responsibility,
sacrifice, and faith.
This thing I possess necessitates a shift
for the sake of my rathe.

A shift in my mind and thoughts, a shift in my habits.
I must become it, transform my palate.

For I am the making and breaking of me.
Because I control my destiny.

*Run*

It may be hard to see the finish line.
It may seem like the win is intangible.
You might feel alone.
You may have started in last place.
Maybe you started in first and lost your momentum.
They probably don't take you seriously.
They may even be laughing at you.
But keep running.

Use the doubt, ridicule, and misjudgment to fuel your fire.
Break the shackles of others' expectations and run.
Build up your speed.
Get into your rhythm.
Press on.

Pass up your self-doubt.
Your fears.
Your pain.
Release your past.
Silence your shame.
And run towards your future.

Remind yourself that you are an extension of The Most High
and what IT doesn't do is play about YOU.
The win is already yours.
Just run.

Love's Target

The internet leads us to believe that love looks like a Disney princess movie and feels like butterfly kisses, tastes like Thanksgiving dinner, sounds like amazing grace, and smells like Baccarat.

So we look for someone to hit our hearts right on the bull's eye with this grand exemplification of love, not ever realizing that even if it's slightly off target, if it's honest and true, you still get points.

It still affects you. Transforms you.

If we stop falling for couple goals and start cultivating something real, in time, we will hit the mark.

Late Night Thoughts

I close my eyes and dream of what could be.

If it never reaches mountains,
at least I experienced the valleys and plains.
So beautiful, so natural.
So organic, these terrains.

I wish I could stop time...
remain in this beautiful place,
for the future may not hold the happy ending
my dreams embrace.

But still I'll wander this road to see what comes to life.
No expectations, no reservations, no conversations.

Just present in the moment.
Our moment in time.

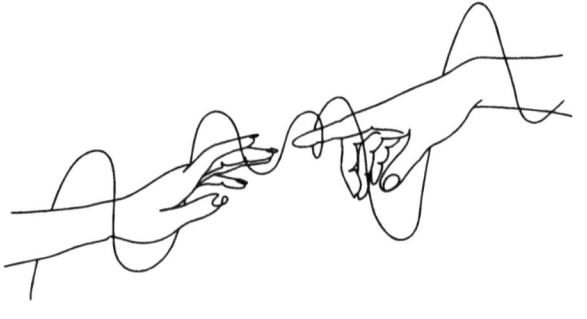

Esoterica

We got this thing.

It's axiomatic (that means obvious)
but enigmatic (mysterious).
So inexplainable... you get it?

Don't know if it's a gift or a curse.
It alarms and intrigues me all at once.
'This thing we have is esoteric', he says.
It's recondite.

But I need more to believe.
For I've given him my body and now I have these
expectations... of which he thinks I've placed too high.
So high, oftentimes he's unwilling to comply.

Contrary to his belief,
I'm not interested in running off into the sunset.
I'd gladly remain in this axiomatic, enigmatic,
invulnerable space.

Exempt from legitimate disappointment,
addicted to the adventure...

My mind in control, our thirst mutual,
and everything is everything.

Influential

The influence she has on him, and he on her,
the influence of strength and optimism.
It marks a beautiful thing.

It shows the value and respect they share,
the eagerness to make each other proud,
the desire to uplift the other when the world tries to tear
them down.

And with their minds combined,
they have the power to change the minds of the
brokenhearted, insecure, damaged beings of this world.

They possess a power so influential, those who care to
spectate are inspired to take just one more step, knock on
one more door, pray one more prayer.

The influence she has on him, and he on her,
the influence of perseverance and synergy.

It marks a beautiful thing.

*Love*

Love is patient. Love is kind.
Love is you and Love is I.

It's beautifully created. In the image of God.
Greatly misunderstood, certainly forgotten.

One thing remains through ups and downs:
Love will sustain when you feel without…

Without a friend, without peace
Love gives joy and eternal increase.

Here's to Love.

Wood Morning

I wake to my head settled on his warm chest.
His arm wrapped around my naked body.

My fingers trace his tattoos until I reach the gray briefs
resting on his hips. Do I wake him for some morning love or
let him rest?

Today I'll be selfish and interrupt his slumber but I
suspect the moment he arises, he'll consider me selfless
and flip me over.

As I presumed, he takes my cue, grabs my hand,
and leads me to the bathroom.

He bends me over.
Gives me exactly what I need to start my day.
The overflow of euphoria leads me to wonder if I love him
or just the way he makes me feel.

We brush our teeth, he kisses my lips.
I express my gratitude by serving him breakfast in bed
and instantly, the time we froze begins again.
Back to reality.

Wood Morning.

I Love You

I love you.
To the moon and back.
Past the stars and galaxies.
With everything I have.
But we can never be.
Until I love me.

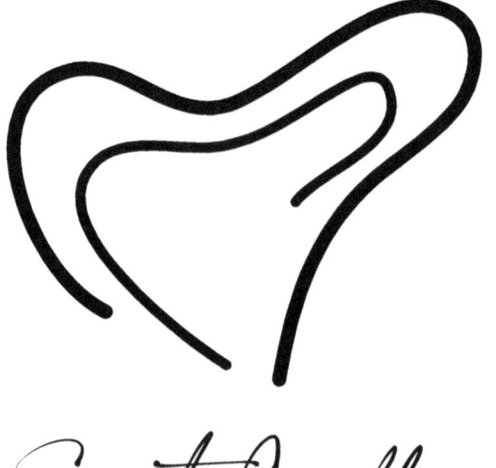

Sweet Goodbye

The kind of goodbye that hurts a little
but bears sweet fruit.

The kind that knows the road has come to an end
but there's excitement about what's ahead.

The kind of goodbye that leaves uncertainty
and a bit of understanding.

A sweet goodbye.

My First Love

My first love.
My first case of butterflies.
My first hope for forever.
My first kiss.
My first time.
The first heart I grew to treasure.

If I could go back in time, I wouldn't.

For you were also my first heartache.
The first lie I believed.
The first tear I cried.
The first time I wished I'd never met someone.

But I love you still, you taught me so much.
How to love myself.
How to put me first.

And for that I'm always grateful.

Becoming

I've yet to become but I love who I'm becoming.

Wiser.
Stronger.
More beautiful.
More focused.

Not where I wish to be but not where I loathe to be.

I'm an intern for this thing called life.
A position I'll hold forever.

For we never stop learning as long as we're living.
And as long as we're living, we're  purpose-fulfilling.
So I work, I pray, I seize the day.
Because I've yet to become but I love who I'm becoming.

More resilient.
More evolved.
More me.

# MEET THE
*Author*

Dondria Fields is a Texas-raised singer, songwriter, actress, fitness enthusiast, and mental health advocate. When she isn't writing music or performing, Dondria enjoys traveling, eating out at vegan restaurants, going to the gym, and dancing the night away. She is also apart of Atlanta Mayor Andre Dickens' Year of The Youth initiative helping to ensure ATL's youth have the tools they need to realize their dreams. This is her first literary work.
Did we mention she loves eating? Because YES.

# Author's Note

Thank you so much for taking the time to read my poetry.

I conceived this collection of poems in the dark, silently functioning with depression and anxiety because I was too ashamed to share that I wasn't ok. I showed up with a smile everyday but inside I was miserable and poetry provided an escape from the real world. It allowed me to process my emotions and then release them.

These poems narrate thoughts I harbored that weren't in alignment with my highest self. These poems describe a life I longed for... if only I could realize I had the power all along to break free from the mental bondage I allowed others to place me in.

**Spoiler Alert** I broke free. Healing is an ongoing process but I'm so proud of where I've landed. As you immerse yourself in these verses, I hope you find solace in knowing that you are not alone in your struggles, and that resilience can bloom even amidst the darkest shadows.

# Keep Up With Dondria

www.dondria.com

www.instagram.com/dondrianicole

www.twitter.com/Dondria

www.facebook.com/OfficialDondria

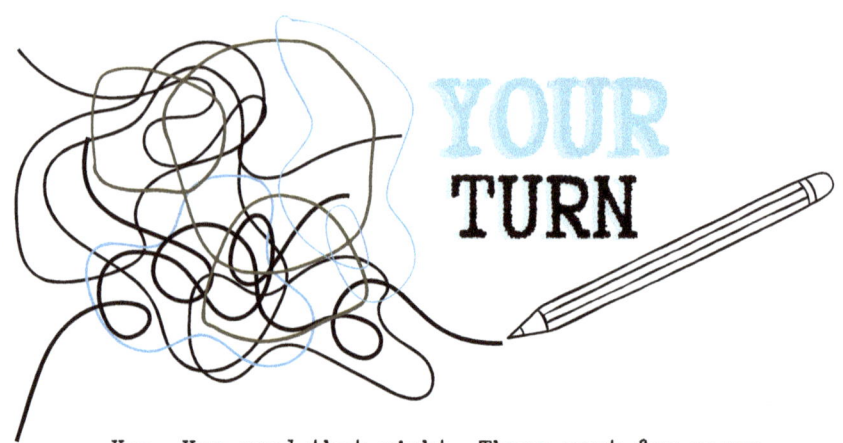

# YOUR TURN

Yep. You read that right. These next few pages are waiting to bear the weight of <u>your</u> thoughts. Let the ink flow like a river, carrying away any negativity that haunts your mind. Not in the mood? Use this space to manifest your dreams or jot down a to-do list for the day.

_____

_____

_____

_____

_____

_____

_____

_____

_____

PERSPECTIVE BY DONDRIA

IS AVAILABLE ON ALL DIGITAL
STREAMING PLATFORMS.